Words That Stretch the Mind and Lift the Spirit

ALSO BY JAMES PHILLIPS NOBLE

*Beyond the Burning Bus:
The Civil Rights Movement in a Southern Town*

*Getting Beyond Tragedy: A Minister's Search to the
'Why God?' Question Which Torments Grieving Families*

Words and Images That Seep into the Soul

Twenty Poems for Those Attaining Three Score and Ten Years

Words That Stretch the Mind and Lift the Spirit

(A Sequel to *Words And Images That Seep into the Soul*)

JAMES PHILLIPS NOBLE

Copyright © 2018 by James Phillips Noble
All rights reserved under International and Pan-American Copyright Conventions. Produced in the United States by NewSouth Books, a division of NewSouth, Inc., Montgomery, Alabama.

ISBN 978-1-60306-987-8

Design by Randall Williams

Printed in the United States of America

*To the family into which I was born,
the family into which I married,
and all the family since then*

Contents

Preface / xiii
Acknowledgments / xvi

Part 1 — Life
The Fathomlessness of Life / 4
Life Is Like a Ship Upon the Sea / 5
The Wealthy Poor / 6
Many Truths / 7
An Authentic Word at Easter Time / 9
Gratitude and Happiness / 10
Children / 11

Part 2 — Christian Experience
The Breath at Pentecost / 14
New Breath / 15
The Truth / 16
The Power of Association / 17
Heart and Spirit / 18
Life: Shallow or Deep / 20
The Significance of Decision / 21
The Infinite Significance of Every Moment / 22
Free Will / 23
Our Yes or No / 24
The Birth of a New Being / 25
Restlessness / 26
The Yank / 27
The Glories That Encircle Us / 28
Choosing the Road to Take / 29
Music in the Heart / 30

Part 3 — Faith
    Hope / 34
    The Answering Grasp / 35
    Hardened Hope and Quickened Faith / 37

Part 4 — Adversities
    Help for Days of Gloom / 40
    Clouds and Stars / 41
    The Blessings of Adversity / 43
    What Cancer Cannot Do / 44

Part 5 — Challenges
    The Road Is Rough / 46
    Goodness in the Face of Evil / 47
    How God Works on the Planet Earth / 48

Part 6 — Prayer
    My Prayer / 52
    A Prayer / 54
    Prayer for the Set of the Heart / 55
    A Wholesome Prayer / 56

Part 7 — God
    The World in God's Hands / 58
    Chance Creation / 59
    The Imagined God / 61
    The Forgiveness of Jesus / 62

Part 8 — Grace and Forgiveness
    Our Sins: The Carrot and the Stick / 64
    Scouring / 65
    The Feathers of God's Wings / 66
    The Consolations of God / 67
    A Blocked Spiritual Artery / 68

Part 9 — Providence
God Will Hold His Children / 70
Reflection at Age Ninety / 71
The Beautiful Fiords of Norway / 72
When I Look at the Starry Heavens / 74
Ample Power to Meet Whatever Comes / 75
The Absent God and the Present God / 76

Part 10 — Christmas
Bethlehem / 78
The Savior's Birth / 81
Christmas Silence / 82
A Christmas Poem for a Violent World / 83
When Jesus Was Born in Bethlehem / 84
A Relevant Comment / 86
Christmas 2016 / 87

Part 11 — Peace
Put Your Touches on My Spirit, O Lord / 90
The Master's Touch / 91

Part 12 — Death and Eternal Life
The Basic Fear / 94
Death / 95
Listen to the Easter Lilly / 96
The Presence of a Loved One / 97
Reflections from the Reality of God's Presence / 98
Reflections from Age Ninety-Six / 99
God's Other Room / 101
There Is a Life to Come / 102
A Little Strip of Sea / 103
The Transition / 104
The Growing Spirit / 106
A Sparkling Moment / 107

Deep Calm / 108
Spirit to Spirit / 109
I Have Lost Myself / 111
Assurance of Grace / 113

Part 13 — Mystery
Mystery / 116
The God-given Sense of Right and Wrong / 118
Prayer and Mystery / 119
Great Is the Mystery of God / 120
On the Edge of Mystery / 121

Part 14 — Character
A Parable / 124
Three Metals / 126

Part 15 — General
The Church Upon the Rock Was Built* / 129
The Limits of Responsibility / 130
A Poem / 132
The Communion of Family and Friends / 133
Darkness and a Tiny Point of Light / 134
Two Consciences / 137
Yearning / 138
Old People Can Grow / 139

Postscript
Reflections by Dr. Frederick Reed / 141

Reflection

Poetry, even free verse, will fall into the crack on the surface of the being, and inspire and lift the spirit.

Prose, which is everywhere, will teach, stretch, and inform the mind on an endless number of topics.

Quotations will keep the wisdom of the past and present before us.

Preface

Words that Stretch the Mind and Lift the Spirit is a collection of original poems or free verse and quotations ancient and modern. All of them come out of the seventy-three years since my ordination.

The poems arose from my deep and rich experiences of pastoral ministry where I dealt with many issues of life, both joyful and sad. I began writing poetry as my family and I dealt with the leukemia that our son Scott had struggled with for a year and a half before he died on a black Saturday, the day before Easter in 1968. He was thirteen years old. The writing then was cathartic for me. In 2005, these poems were published in a book, *Getting Beyond Tragedy: A Minister's Search to the 'Why God?' Question Which Torments Grieving Families*.

I never stopped writing poems after Scott died. In 2013, Wipf and Stock published a book of my poetry and selected quotations, *Words and Images That Seep into the Soul*. I am encouraged by the way many readers have used the book in their devotional lives. The present book, *Words that Stretch the Mind and Lift the Spirit*, is a sequel to the earlier one. Both books had the same origin and motivation for writing.

I GRADUATED FROM high school in Raymond, Mississippi, in 1939. World War II had already begun in Europe and the clear feeling in America was that we would enter the war before too long. I had decided that I wanted to go into the ministry of the Presbyterian Church. My financial resources from a sharecropper's farm were very limited. Presbyterian colleges were expensive and beyond my reach, even with a small denominational scholarship. In our search, we found King College in Bristol, Tennessee. It had fewer than three hundred students and was struggling to survive. When Pearl Harbor came in 1941, and America entered the war, many young men were drafted, including two of my brothers. I was deferred, as were all who were preparing for the ministry, based on the idea that chaplains would be needed. Many, including me, wanted to speed up their college and seminary as much as possible. I went straight through college, including the summers.

After three years, I lacked only ten hours to graduate. Most colleges required that the last year had to be taken at the college. The Presbyterian seminaries had a strict policy that students must have a college degree before being accepted. I approached King College about permitting me to get my last ten credits at some other college. I also approached the president of Columbia Theological Seminary about entering the seminary before I got my college degree. I thought this might be possible, as many things were being sped up because of the war; still, I was pleasantly surprised when these arrangements were accepted.

When I graduated from seminary in the spring of 1945, the year the war ended, I had the sense that my education was neither complete nor as good as it might have been if not for the war. Then an intriguing thing happened at the seminary graduation. The president of Emory University was the speaker, and I was vividly struck by one thing he said. It was quite simple: "Keep growing!" That became an inspiration, especially during the earlier years of my ministry, but it continued through all my ministry. This motivated my reading as widely as I could, in depth in the Christian religion and theology, but also in other fields. My determination to "keep growing" led me to a stimulating year in England, at Cambridge University, after I had already spent twenty-six years in the ministry.

In Anniston, Alabama, where I was a minister for fifteen years, an elder in the church moved away and left a full set of *Great Books of the Western World* to the church library. Over time I read quite extensively in these books. It was then that I developed the practice of marking out short passages that struck me as having special meaning and giving them to my secretary to type and put in a file. Over many years of ministry, I accumulated quite a large number of files.

Later, I conceived the idea of a book of quotations and free verse poetry that I had written over the decades, titled *Words and Images That Seep into the Soul*. This new volume is a sequel, with quotations from the many files I had accumulated and free verse and other writing I have done, mostly after the first book.

My sense of not having had the best education was a motivation for both volumes. Although there were other motivations, the imperative to "keep growing" was consistently there.

Acknowledgments

As most of the included quotations and poems are related to my life experiences, I am reminded that many people have touched my life for good. I am grateful to them, especially Popesy, my wife for sixty-seven years, and my three children, Betty, Phil Jr., and Scott.

In the earlier days of my ministry my longtime devoted secretary, Mary Catherine White, was responsible for typing and filing quotations from my reading that I thought were significant. The result was a number of files from over the years, and from those I have chosen the quotations in this book as well as the quotations from my earlier book, *Words and Images That Seep into the Soul*.

I am very grateful to Megan Jarboe for her careful typing and editing of the manuscript. She is an Agnes Scott College graduate and has been a valued administrative assistant to my daughter for many years. More recently, she has become special in my life as well.

Finally, I am indebted to Randall Williams, editor of NewSouth Books, which has previously published two of my books. His skill is reflected in each of my books that NewSouth has published.

I am grateful for the many people by whom I have been blessed through the years of my long life.

Words That Stretch the Mind and Lift the Spirit

Part 1

Life

The Fathomlessness of Life

We keep probing deeply to find life's full meaning.
As science, religion, philosophy, and astrology searches
Knowledge, awareness, and insight
Seeps into the sides of our well of inquiry.
We go deeper and more seeps in.
The deeper we go the more slowly
New information seeps in.
But we do make a discovery.
We learn that there is a
Fathomlessness to the ultimate full meaning of life.

October 15, 2009

Thoughts stirred by *Now and Then* by Frederick Buechner, page 108.

Life Is Like a Ship Upon the Sea

Life is like a ship upon the sea.
There are days when the weather is fine.
The sun shines brightly and the waters are calm.
There are days when storms make the water rough
And the ship is tossed about.
As the ship approaches the harbor,
When it is securely anchored
The passengers disembark.
They have reached their destination.

August 25, 2014

The Wealthy Poor

> *"Fear not, my son, that we are made poor;*
> *For thou hast much wealth,*
> *If thou fear God and depart from all sins,*
> *And do that which is pleasing in his sight."*
> —Apocrypha Tobit 4:21

Wealth is not to be despised,
Whether it is external or internal wealth.
A measure of external wealth
Can make life so much better,
And we can be grateful for it.

But there are many things it cannot do,
And it can be taken from us—lost.
In our lack of external wealth
We may miss the fact
That there is internal wealth.

Faith in God, a clear conscience,
And an endeavoring to do God's will
Is a wealth that can do
Many things that external wealth cannot do,
And it is a wealth that cannot be taken away.

November 3, 2010

Many Truths

By Patricia (Pat) Boinest Potter*

There are many truths.

We each write our own
My first truth was my father
My first lesson was trust.

Our house was always full
Of love and laughter.
Love of each other
Love of beauty
Love of art
Love of architecture
Love of animals
Love of plants
Love of the world
Love of God.

Our house was always full
Of friends, family, and workers
From my father's architecture firm
Behind the house.
Whoever happened to be there at lunchtime
Came to the big house for lunch.
Clients, carpenters, contractors, draughtsmen,
My sister and me.

My mother's twin sisters
Lived with us
Their boyfriends were around.
Adding to the fullness
Of love and laughter

My father died when I was twelve.
One of my many truths
Is that death is a part of life.

There is a conscious energy that never dies
An energy imprinted by a life
That passes into a multi-dimensional space
Layered with ours so that our beloved
Are always right here with us.

I learned early
There are many ways
Of becoming
Of being,
Of disappearing . . .

I learned later
There are many layered dimensions
Of truth
Of reality
Of life

". . . and the greatest of these is LOVE"

*Pat is a longtime artist and dear friend from Anniston, Alabama, whose art and writing have provided much insight and inspiration over the years.

An Authentic Word at Easter Time

By Patricia (Pat) Boinest Potter

The role that religion has played in my life keeps changing. Through my first forty years I never missed a Sunday in Church. In my early thirties, I started a practice of a different kind of Meditation that I did every day, not just on Sunday. I began Traveling and met people from different lands who had been Raised in different ways and realized that there are many different Ways to be, to think about God and about life. Now, for me, God is a constant presence.

The nanosecond didn't exist when I was a child. The world has Gotten so much smaller. Communication, TVs, computers, etc. Have changed its size. Just in the last year I have learned about Dark matter and dark energy, what we used to look at and call Space. Dark energy causes the universe to expand and dark matter Holds it together. What we call *God* is in all of this and each of us Is a part. Life is about finding and playing your part, your way to *Play*, to *enjoy!* To *be!!!*

We celebrate Easter as a day of resurrection, a day of new life And renewal. I thank GOD for the life of Jesus, whose life gives Us stories, passed down through the ages, of how GOD can live In woman and man.

March 24, 2018

Gratitude and Happiness

Gratitude is basic to happiness.
Not just saying thanks for this or that,
But the deep feeling of gratitude.
When the attitude of the spirit
Is that of gratefulness
Then happiness can occur.
Without the deep feeling of gratitude,
Happiness will be elusive.

October 3, 2014

Children

By Forest E. Witcraft*

A hundred years from now
It will not matter what my
Bank account was, the sort
Of house I lived in or the kind
Of car I drove—but the
World may be different because
I was important in the life
      Of a child.**

*Teacher and Scholar

**This poem hung in my daughter Betty's psychology office, where she worked with children for thirty years.

Part 2

Christian Experience

The Breath at Pentecost

Pentecost was the moment in which the new Breath which was Breathed into them drove out all the poisonous fumes of negative self-images they had unwittingly inhaled from the milieu. Blessed is the man who is poor in or free from the inhalations of false attitudes toward himself. Cursed is the man who is rich in lies about his own identity. The joy of the kingdom belongs to those to whom it has been given to inhale the truth about himself.

From *The Lord of the Journey*, page 160.

New Breath

God created man and breathed into him the breath of life.
Jesus redeems life that is filled with sin.
The Holy Spirit at Pentecost breathed new life
Which energized the disciples for the kingdom of God.

That same Holy Spirit still breathes new life
Into men and women in today's world.
Now and again the Spirit breathes
On a puzzled and seeking teenager
Who has not yet found his way.
And that breath clears away the debris
That has accumulated in his growing and inquiring mind.
He then sees a way emerging that leads him
Through the uncharted forest of his future.

Breathe on all of us, O God,
That we may see the way
That takes us through this
complicated and dangerous world.

February 7, 2014

The Truth

Somehow the truth is breaking through,
Like spilled ink.
It colors my mind,
It shapes my character,
It penetrates my spirit,
It changes the surface me
And reaches the deep within.

In its breaking through
I begin to understand
That knowing the truth
Is making me free.

December 9, 2013

The Power of Association

Who has not said of someone
He is just like his father, or
She reminds me of her mother.
It is not just a matter of genes.
It is also a matter of association.
Parent and child have lived together
And that relationship has resulted in some similarity.

When someone knows the stories
Of the life, death, and resurrection of Jesus,
And has faith in Jesus,
Then the association with Jesus
Results in a manner of thinking and living
So that someone may say
He or she is a Christian.

November 9, 2009

Heart and Spirit

> *"Create in me a clean heart, O God,
> and renew a right spirit within me."*
> — Psalm 51:10

If I have a heart of stone
Then create in me a new heart.
If I have been given a new heart,
But in the ordinary living of life
It has become unclean
As it has been bombarded by
Envy, jealousy, covetousness,
Anger, pride, and doubt,
So my heart needs to be cleaned.
As I bathe my body each day,
So my heart needs to be cleaned each day.

And my spirit? It gets worn down.
Life isn't always like I want it to be.
Disappointment strikes hard at my spirit.
I get tired of trying,
And the light in my spirit
Dims and sometimes flickers.
Let me sense anew
The gift of God's grace.
Let me hear again the promises of God.
Then my spirit is quickened.

With a clean heart, and a renewed spirit,
I can move forward
With a deepened sense of joy
Which is deeper than superficial happiness.
And my life looks and feels different.

November 5, 2009

Life: Shallow or Deep

By Paul Tillich*

Look at the student who knows the content of the Hundred most important books of world history, and yet whose spiritual life remains as shallow as it ever was, or perhaps becomes even more superficial. And then look at an uneducated worker who performs a mechanical task day by day, but who suddenly asks himself, "What does it mean, that I do this work? What does it mean for my life? What is the meaning of my life?" Because he asks these questions, that man is on the way into depth, whereas the other man, the student of history, dwells on the surface among petrified bodies, brought out of the depth by some spiritual earthquake of the past. The simple worker may grasp truth, even though he cannot answer his questions; the learned scholar may possess no truth, even though he knows all the truths of the past.

*From *The Shaking of the Foundations*, page 55.

The Significance of Decision

By Soren Kierkegaard*

"Come hither!" Oh, stand not still, considering
The matter. Consider rather, oh consider that
For every instant thou standest still after hearing
the invitation, thou will in the next instant hear
its call fainter and fainter, and thus be withdrawing
to a distance though thou be standing at the same spot.

*From *Training in Christianity*

The Infinite Significance of Every Moment

By Paul Tillich*

The infinite significance of every moment of time is this: In it We decide, and are decided about, with respect to our eternal future.

*From *The Shaking of the Foundations*, page 37.

Free Will

By John Calvin*

What *free will* is, though the expression frequently occurs in all writers, few have defined. Yet Origen appears to have advanced a position to which they all assented, when he calls it a power of *reason* to discern good and evil, of *will* to choose either. Nor does Augustine differ from him, when he teaches that it is a power of reason and will, by which good is chosen when grace assists; and evil, when grace is wanting.

*From *Calvin's Institutes*, Vol. 1, page 284.

Our Yes or No

By Lewis Joseph Sherrill[*]

In any case the self is confronted by the living God not once only, but an endless number of times during his pilgrimage from infancy onward. In each of these confrontations he must answer with his "Yes" or his "No." Perhaps this fact of the continuing encounter offers the reason why the Bible has so little to say about conversion, and so much to say about repentance; for repentance is a "change of mind."

[*]From *The Gift of Power*, pages 161–162.

The Birth of a New Being

By Lewis Joseph Sherrill*

The principle of insight is of great importance in situations where moral and spiritual confusion prevail. Into such a situation a ray of light may flash, to be followed perhaps by the feeling which one expresses when he says, "Now *this* makes *sense*." Or it may be followed by a sense of being released to pursue some goal without being held back. At times the flash of insight will light up a relatively small field with the new meaning for the self who perceives it. At other times the insight will penetrate so far into the total field in which the self is involved as to cause one to feel that he has entered "a new world." And at still other times the new insight will cause a shift within the self so radical as to give one the feeling and the conviction that a new self is coming into being.

When insight is followed by the feeling of seeing a new world or of being a new and different self, we are at the threshold of those "deeper changes in the self." Indeed, one who uses such terms concerning himself probably is undergoing changes of a much deeper kind than those which we commonly refer to as "learning." The precise language of a quantitative psychology becomes less and less capable of expressing what is happening. One is obliged to turn instead to the symbolic language of poetry, music, art, and religion for terms with which he can communicate the subtleties of the new meaning.

*From *The Gift of Power*, pages 155–156.

Restlessness

Thoughts stirred by a poem by George Herbert

When God first made man
He gave him almost everything.
The garden of fruit trees and vines,
So he could eat and drink and be merry,
And walk in the cool of the shade
In the beauty of the garden.
God gave him wisdom, honor, and pleasure.
And God called it good.

But God did not give him everything.
God did not give him peace and rest.
God said man may love
The things that I have given him
And not the ONE who gave them.

If the goodness of God in giving
Rich blessings does not lead man to God,
Then maybe restlessness will lead him to God.

"Our souls are restless until they find rest in God."

March 27, 2014

The Yank

I lie in bed thinking.
My life takes up the space of a few years.
Only God has no beginning and no end.
My heart has been filled with many things,
Good things and some not so good.
But all of them will pass away
Even as will my body of clay.

God has set eternity in the heart of man.*
That eternity is God's living eternal spirit.
I pray: Open my heart to your Spirit, God.
Then I shall be touched with eternity,
And as the temporal things pass away,
My spirit, touched and claimed by eternity,
Will be with God forever and forever.

But if in my sinful humanity and short-sightedness
I close tight the door of my heart,
Then, God, yank it open and enter,
So that having filled my heart
With your eternal Spirit,
I will live forever with You
And all kindred spirits.

October 9, 2009

*Ecclesiastes 3:11

The Glories That Encircle Us

*Thoughts stirred by a poem by T. Whytehead**

Sometimes it seems like a curtain
Has been thrown over eternal things.
But now and then a corner of the curtain
Is lifted and we glimpse
The glories that encircle us.

May 22, 2014

*In "*Five Minutes a Day*," by Robert E. Speer, page 247.

Choosing the Road to Take

Two roads merged in a woods . . .
But today six or more merge in the woods.
Choosing the one to take is difficult.
One seems to be less traveled.
Another one is wide with many travelers.
Another leads to mountains
Where traveling is difficult.
Another road is narrow
With a ditch on both sides.
Another road leads to a desert
Where oases are few and far between.
Another road leads through the swamps
Where dangerous creatures live.
Another road leads downward
Where the going seems to be easy.

I stand where they all intersect,
And I must choose one.
As I look down each one.
I cannot see very far.
I do not know what is beyond.
With the best intelligence I have
And with faith by which
God may show me the road to choose,
I choose one and go with a leap of faith.

August 17, 2014

Music in the Heart

The cares of the world are with us.
Multitudes with hunger day and night.
Violence greater than can be imagined.
Hate that drifts like clouds
And now and then suddenly sends
Piercing lightning
And loud rolling thunder.

There is the turbulence of daily life
Bringing the ups and downs
Of human experience.
Anxiety. A child is wandering.
The future is dusky.
Choices are made.
Are they good and wise decisions?
Living brings relationships,
Some easy and happy,
Others difficult and stressful.

The human spirit has layers.
There is the surface layer.
On this level we deal
With the issues of daily living.
There is a deeper level
Where the mind and spirit
Reacts to the crosscurrents
That occur in every life.

There is still a deeper level.
Beyond the care of the world
And the pleasant and unpleasant
Minutiae of daily living
Where the essence of the soul is reached.
At that depth, what is there?
Is it hollow or empty?
Or do we discover that something
Is there? Listen! Do you hear
A soft and distant music?
Could it be the music
Of the morning stars singing together,
Or the music of the spheres?

That music reaches our depths
And becomes a part of us.
We live with this music
Of the universe in our hearts.
Our secret soul absorbs
The music of eternity
Which is with us always.
So we live with this music in our hearts.

May 6, 2014

Part 3

Faith

Hope

When I experience some of the downs of daily life and feel
the stress and strains that are heavy on my spirit,
and when my soul thinks of it . . .

. . . and is bowed down within me.
But this I call to mind, and therefore I have hope.

The steadfast love of the Lord never ceases,
His mercies never come to an end;
They are new every morning;
Great is thy faithfulness.
"The Lord is my portion," says my soul,
"Therefore I will hope in him."

The Lord is good to those who wait for him,
To the soul who seeks him.
It is good that one should wait quietly
For the salvation of the Lord.*

November 16, 2012

*Lamentations 3:20–26

The Answering Grasp

> *"Our souls are restless*
> *Until they find rest in God."*
>
> — Isobel Kuhn*

Our restlessness may be a good thing.
It may cause us to reach out
For something beyond us
For an answer to satisfy our restlessness.
The search is finished in one sense
When our hand, stretched out to God
In the name of his appointed
Mediator Jesus Christ,
Feels the answering grasp
And knows God is there.

How do we know when
There is an answering grasp?
When we reach out our hand
For a handshake we know
When there is an answering grasp.
The touch of flesh is felt.
At the same time there is
Something else that is felt.
It is the intangible mind to mind,
Spirit to spirit.
Therefore we can say,

It is a cold handshake or a warm handshake.
That does not refer to the physical touch,
But to the intangible spirit to spirit.

So when we reach out in spirit or soul
To God in the name of God's
Appointed mediator, Jesus Christ,
We may sense the answering grasp
Of the Spirit and know that God is there.

The reality of that grasp is the beginning.
This is the first discovery of the answering grasp
With the sense that God is there.
It will be followed by another and another
And so it goes on and on.
It is never ended but each answering grasp
Is more thrilling as we explore just who
It is that is there with the answering grasp.

June 26, 2014

*Quoted in *The Lord of the Journey*, page 283.

Hardened Hope and Quickened Faith

Hope is a projection into the future.
Sometimes it is a faint hope,
And then again it is a lively hope.

Faith gives substance to hope.
But faith sometimes is dimmed
And then again it glows brightly.

Bright faith makes hope
Harden into steel.
Lord, brighten my faith
And harden my hope.

November 5, 2009

Part 4

Adversities

Help for Days of Gloom

"Into each life some rain must fall,
Some days must be dark and dreary."
— Henry Wordsworth Longfellow

There will be times when our spirits are low,
We feel dull, cold and dreary,
When the light within is dim,
The mists are thick,
And the sleet begins to fall,
And into our spirits a dark and dull mood
Creeps in and threatens to stay.

Is there a way to warm the spirit?
Is there a way to let the sunlight in?
Is there a way to lift the gloom?
A bit of wisdom from an eighteenth-century bishop:
"When you find yourself overpowered
As it were by melancholy,
The best way is to go out,
And do something kind to somebody."*

February 11, 2010

---

*Bishop Francis Paget in *The Spirit of Discipline (1891)*; quoted in *A Diary of Readings* by John Baille Day, page 110.

Clouds and Stars

> *"I have not known a day without a cloud,*
> *Nor have I known a night without a star."*
> — J. Ritche Smith

In our youth we look forward,
When before us is the cloud of unknowing.
We dream, we aspire as there are many roads
To choose from.
Where each road leads we do not know,
And we choose with hope and anxiety.

In our older years we look backward
Over the long way the kindly years have led us.
Along the way there have been clouds.
Some small and white and clearly drifting away.
Some large and dark stretching across the sky,
And they are moving slowly.
They have brought rain
And sometimes lightning and wind,
And loud scary claps of thunder.

When the somber and threatening clouds leave,
And the night comes, we see the stars.
The stars are always there.
The North Star, bright and constant, is
In the same place it has been for eons,
Like the everlasting love of God

That shines in our spirits bringing
Faith and hope.

The radiant dawn has brought our day.
The sunset comes and is as radiant as the dawn.
When our day is done
The sinking and disappearing sun
Colors the sky over the western horizon
With varying shades of red and gold.
When it disappears in the dark
Then the lights of heaven appear.

April 15, 2014

The Blessings of Adversity

Solzhenitsyn said: "It was only when
I lay there on rotting prison straw
That I sensed within myself
The first stirrings of good.
It nourished my soul there and
I say, 'Bless you, prison,
For having been in my life.'"*

Not all adversities bring blessings.
But there may be times
When the experience of adversity
Does bring some unexpected blessings.
God works in mysterious ways.
For Solzhenitsyn, spending some time
In prison on rotting straw
He felt the first stirrings of good.
So significant was that that it led
Him to say, "Bless you, prison,
For having been in my life."

Have we had the experience of an adversity
That brought some significant blessings to us?

September 30, 2014

**The Lord of the Journey*, page 339.

What Cancer Cannot Do

By Robert L. Lynn*

Cancer is so limited . . .
It cannot cripple love;
It cannot shatter hope;
It cannot corrode faith;
It cannot eat away peace;
It cannot destroy friendship;
It cannot kill confidence;
It cannot shut out memories;
It cannot silence courage;
It cannot invade the soul;
It cannot reduce eternal life;
It cannot quench God's Spirit;
It cannot lessen the
        Power of the Resurrection.

*Copied—Dr. John Cave.

Part 5

Challenges

The Road Is Rough

> *"The road is rough, our Father.*
> *But we are not dismayed,*
> *For we are more than earth and dust.*
> *We are akin to Thee,*
> *Who has made us in Thine image."*
> — ROBERT E. SPEER, from *Five Minutes a Day*

> *"The real glory is being knocked to your knees,*
> *And then coming back. That is real glory.*
> *That is the essence of it."*
> — VINCE LOMBARDI

The road of life is rough and hard.
It is not smooth and easy,
But the challenge of navigating it
Produces character.
A good perspective on who we are
Is helpful and gives us stamina.
We are earthly creatures
And often covered with earthly dust.
But we are more than earth and dust.
We are kin to God,
For God has made us in his own image.
And that kinship tells us
That we, all of us, are part of the Royal Family.

February 17, 2014

Goodness in the Face of Evil

During World War II the small French town of Le Chambon became a refuge for Jews who were trying to escape the German Nazis who were taking men, women and children to death camps. The town, made up mostly of Protestant Huguenots, welcomed refugees because of their reverence of life. They risked their lives to help the persecuted Jews who were being killed by the millions by Hitler's gestapo.

The author of the book telling the story of human goodness in the face of unbelievable evil concludes with this paragraph:

"I, who share Trocme's (the leader of Le Chambon's becoming a refuge) and the Chambonnais' belief in the preciousness of human life, may never have the moral strength to be much like the Chambonnais or like Trocme; but I know that I want to have a door in the depths of my being, a door that is not locked against the faces of all other human beings. I know that I want to be able to say, from those depths, 'Naturally, come in, and come in.'"*

May 4, 2016

---

*From *Lest Innocent Blood Be Shed* by Philip Hallie, page 287.

How God Works on the Planet Earth

God does God's work on the planet earth
Through God's highest creation—human beings.
When God gets ready to do something,
Great or small, God lets a baby be born.

There are examples that stand out.
When each example is named
Our minds fill up with their accomplishments.
To name a few out of thousands:
Abraham, Moses, David, the twelve apostles,
Augustine, Martin Luther, John Calvin, John Knox,
Abraham Lincoln and Winston Churchill and Mother Teresa.
There are many others who were used by God,
To bring about God's will on earth.
There are millions and millions of unknown people
Who were called to do some part
Of what God wanted done on earth.
Scratch around in these millions
And you will find your name there.

Above all, when God wanted to redeem mankind
A baby was born in a stable in Bethlehem.
God announced that amazing birth
By the songs of a band of angels
And the worship of a few humble shepherds,
And by the brilliant star in the sky
That led three wise men to the manger
Where the baby Jesus lay on the hay.

Jesus' teachings, his life, death, and resurrection
have altered the lives of millions of people.
And, of course, every single one was born a baby.
God had a purpose for each life.
When we were born God had a purpose for each of us.
Each of us has a part, large or small,
In doing what God wants to happen
On the planet called earth.

Think about it! Think about it!
God has chosen each of us
To have some part in doing
What God wants to be done on earth.

That God has chosen you and me
To have a part in what he wants done
On the planet earth
May be the highest honor
That any of us will ever receive.

December 1, 2012

Part 6

Prayer

My Prayer

Spirit___Spirit of gentleness,
Spirit___Spirit of tenderness,
Spirit___Spirit of quietness,
    Gently blow into my spirit;
    Quietly seep into my soul.

Spirit___Spirit of faithfulness,
Spirit___Spirit of hopefulness,
Spirit___Spirit of loveliness,
    Gently blow into my spirit;
    Quietly seep into my soul.

Spirit___Spirit of peacefulness,
Spirit___Spirit of comfortness,
Spirit___Spirit of joyfulness,
    Gently blow into my spirit;
    Quietly seep into my soul.

Spirit___Spirit of thankfulness,
Spirit___Spirit of gratefulness,
Spirit___Spirit of wonderfulness,
        Gently blow into my spirit;
        Quietly seep into my soul.

Spirit___Spirit of mercifulness,
Spirit___Spirit of kindliness,
Spirit___Spirit of prayerfulness,
        Gently blow into my spirit;
        Quietly seep into my soul.

May 23, 2013

A Prayer

Eternal God, who loving us has saved us;
Who having made us does understand us;
Who calling us does challenge us;
Who redeeming us does keep us;
    but we feel thy love by which we are saved;
    let us realize that you understand us completely;
    let us hear your call which challenges us;
    let us live in the confidence of
        your keeping power.
We pray in the name of Jesus, who is our Savior and Lord.
Amen.

July 21, 1957

Prayer for the Set of the Heart

St. Thomas Aquinas (1225–1274)*

Give me, O Lord:

A steadfast heart,
Which no unworthy affection may drag downward.

An unconquered heart,
Which no tribulation can wear out.

An upright heart,
Which no unworthy purpose may tempt aside.

From *Prayers Ancient and Modern*, page 42.

A Wholesome Prayer

By Robert E. Speer*

We pray thee, give us:

Our daily work that
We may earn our daily bread.

A little hardship that
We may grow lusty souls.

A little sorrow that
Our tears may run for others' grief.

A little task that
We may do for thee to make our journey worthwhile.

*Abridged, from *Five Minutes a Day*.

Part 7

God

The World in God's Hands

The children sang:
"He's got the whole world in His hands."
Picture that!

God's outstretched hands
Holding the planet earth.
The beautiful earth of God's creation,
The mountains, hills and valleys,
The streams, lakes and oceans,
The verdant green of trees and plants.
And God is pleased.

And on earth, there is God's highest creation,
Human beings, man and woman
Made in His very own image.
And God's heart throbs with love.

But God's hands are pricked
By the violence of
Man's inhumanity to man.
The swords, guns, and bombs,
And as they inflict pain and death,
The hurt is felt in God's hands.
It is not the pricks in God's hands
But the pain in God's heart of love and compassion
That causes a tear to drop from God's eyes.

November 22, 2009

Chance Creation

By Stanley Jones*

The situation is clearing for the modern man. He sees more and more that he must affirm some "yes" about the universe, and that "yes" may be God. For how could this universe come by chance into a cosmic orderliness that stretches from the molecule to the outermost star, and controls everything between? And how could this orderliness just happen to stay by chance through millions of years? That would be a stark materialistic miracle—universal chaos by chance gives birth to universal order! The one who believes that must spell his "chance" with a capital "C" and mean by it—God. How long do you think it would take for you to throw up a font of type into the air and have it come down by chance into a poem of Browning? I asked a printer that question and he replied, "Both you and the type would wear out first."

Someone has figured out how many chances to one it would take for the world to have happened by chance, and the figures go round the world thirty-five times for it to have happened by chance. "A preposterous figure," says Dr. Millikan the scientist. Sir James Jeans has figured out that it would take a hundred million years for a hundred thousand monkeys, pecking at random on a hundred thousand typewriters, to happen by chance upon the plays of Shakespeare. And then, after they had happened upon the arrangement of the letters, they wouldn't know what the letters meant!

When I pick up a book and see that there is intelligence in

it—that sometimes does happen!—then I know that behind that intelligence is an intelligent mind expressing itself through that intelligence. When I look at the universe, I find that it responds to intelligence—it can be intelligently studied. Intelligence has gone into it—into its very structure. Then the simple conclusion must be that behind that intelligence, which is built into the structure of things, is an intelligent mind, and since that built-in intelligence seems to be universal, I will have to spell it in capitals—A Universal Mind.

*From *Abundant Living*, page 5.

The Imagined God

By John Calvin*

The true state of the case is that the mind of man, being full of pride and temerity, dares to conceive of God according to its own standard; and, being sunk in stupidity, and immersed in profound ignorance, imagines a vain and ridiculous phantom instead of God.

*From *Calvin's Institutes of the Christian Religion*, vol. 1, pages 122–123.

The Forgiveness of Jesus

By Fyodor Dostoevsky*

. . . You said just now, is there a being in the whole world who would have the right to forgive and could forgive? But there is a Being and He can forgive everything, all and for all, because he gave his innocent blood for all and everything. You have forgotten Him, and on Him is built the edifice, and it is to Him they cry aloud, "Thou art just, O Lord, for Thy ways are revealed."

*From chapter 5, *The Brothers Karamazov*.

Part 8

Grace and Forgiveness

Our Sins: The Carrot and the Stick

Rust accumulates on metal
And restricts the purpose for which it was made.
Sins are like rust on our souls.
Tribulations serve to scour off
The rust of our sins.*

God's kindness comes to us in many ways.
We call them blessings.
How vast is the sum of them!**
Sometimes we wonder
Why God is so good to us.
God's kindness is meant
To lead us to repentance.***
In true repentance our sins are forgiven.

September 26, 2009

**The Imitation of Christ* by Thomas A. Kempis, page 262.
**Psalm 139:17.
***Romans 2:4.

Scouring

> *Tribulations serves to scour off the rust of our sins.*
> — Thomas A. Kempis*

A soft cloth can wipe the dust away.
But sometimes it takes scouring
To get rid of deep stains.

Scouring is an old word;
Like scouring the kitchen floor.
A penetrating cleaner,
And a stiff brush,
And scrubbing back and forth
Until the floor is clean.
That is scouring.

Some of our sins have been with us so long,
That they have formed rust on or in us.
To remove the rust takes scouring.
Could it be that tribulations can serve
To scour off the rust of our sins?

September 20, 2010

*Prayers Ancient and Modern, page 262.

The Feathers of God's Wings

Thoughts stirred by the words of John Donne*

Behold, the mercy of God!
God's mercy like God's love
Is from everlasting to everlasting.
Under God's wings of mercy
refuge is found.
God's feathered wings of mercy
Are spread over the world.
God's mercy is broad
and wide and deep.

There are times when one
Feels the particular mercy of God:
When a heavy burden is lifted,
When a tragedy is averted,
When a sickness is cured,
When joy is deep,
When love is aglow,
When lost hope is regained,
When a ray of light is seen in darkness.

These and many others
Are particular mercies of God.
They are the gentle touch
Of the soft feathers of God's wings.

July 13, 2010

*In *A Diary of Readings* by John Ballie Day, page 235.

The Consolations of God

Theme: Why are you cast down?
                                PSALM 94:17–19, 22

When the cares of my heart are many,
Thy consolations cheer my soul.
                                        PSALM 94:19

She was in the hospital. The operation was not to have been really serious, but the doctor inadvertently punctured something that made the situation very threatening. She was cast down indeed! She was a strong Christian and was knowledgeable about the Bible. As she struggled to handle this she asked for help in finding resources that would give her strength of spirit to get through her difficult and trying time. There are many scripture verses that tell of the consolations of God and she knew many of them, but she needed someone to reassure her and help her grasp God's consolations. Van Dyke, in speaking to a group of students preparing for Christian ministry, said: "Remember, everyone you meet is fighting a hard battle." Maybe not all you meet are having a hard battle at that particular time, but many are, and they need someone to encourage them and help them to find the consolations of God.

Prayer: O God, help us to be sensitive to those who might need help in experiencing the consolations of God. Amen.

                                                        January 12, 2006

A Blocked Spiritual Artery

When the flow of life
Gets clogged up in our spiritual artery,
It can lead to serious trouble.

The spiritual artery can get clogged
When the rubbish of daily life
Accumulates until it forms a mass.
A condition that causes a mass to form
Is the lack of forgiveness.
A daily dose of a forgiving spirit
Helps to keep the mass from forming.
But once the artery gets clogged,
It takes a hard and difficult
Experience of deep forgiveness
To remove the obstructing mass
And to get a healthy flow of spiritual life
Flowing again.

September 20, 2010

Part 9

Providence

God Will Hold His Children

By George McDonald*

Such is the mercy of God that God will hold his children . . . until they drop and purge the selfishness with all the dross that is in it, and rush home to the Father and the Son and many brethren, into the center of life.

*In *The Lord of the Journey*, page 347.

Reflection at Age Ninety

Through all my years I feel I was led
By a gentle providence,
And now my gratitude deepens
every day.

August 5, 2011

The Beautiful Fiords of Norway

We experienced the beautiful fiords of Norway.
The crystal waters reflected the majestic mountains
That surrounded them.
We went to fiord after fiord,
Connected by ferry boats.
While waiting for a ferry
I walked along a path that
Followed the shore line.
I reveled in the beauty all around,
And felt the joy of being
Among the beautiful fiords of Norway.

I walked to the water's edge
And stooped down on the large stones
In order to put my hand in the cold waters,
To feel what I had been seeing.
Being unaware that the stones were slippery
All at once I fell into the fiord!
The reason the ferry boats
Could come to the water's edge
Was because the rock-lined
Shore had no slope to it,
But sharply went straight down
To a great depth.
Having on winter clothes and heavy shoes
There was no way I could swim.
I found myself standing on a protruding rock
About five feet down in water up to my waist.

I fully realized I was in great danger.
I took off my cap and carefully placed it on the
Slippery stone that had caused me to fall into the fiord
So that if I did lose my footing and drown,
It would give a clue to those searching for me.
Then I very carefully reached out
And grasped the stones on the water's edge
And pulled myself out of the fiord.

As I safely sat on the solid ground
I was flooded with a strong sense of gratitude
That the protruding rock was there.
It was a solid rock providentially there
That saved my life.

Thanks be to God
Who has given us
A solid rock of steadfast love
That endures forever
And faith and trust on which
We can stand as we face
The dangers and perils of life.

"On Christ the solid rock I stand,
All other ground is sinking sand."*

April 16, 2014

*Hymn: "My Hope Is Built on Nothing Less"

When I Look at the Starry Heavens

When I look at the starry heavens I am struck by its vastness. It is filled with stars that move in orderly orbits. I sense that in and behind and through the stars there is something, a power or force that fills the space between the stars.

When I look back at my life of ninety-six years, I recognize there have been numberless events, and each one like a star in the heavens. Then I sense that the spaces have been filled with something dynamic. That dynamic is the God who fills all the spaces. And that God has been good and loving.

My marriage—how did it come about? A wife so special and wonderful for sixty-seven years. Three fine children, the opportunities of service that I have had, and the broad travels over six continents. I never dreamed that all of this would come to pass in my life. But the force and dynamic which has brought all these blessings is God who silently fills our lives and makes our dreams come true.

There are still events to come and God's grace and love, and God's dynamic will be in each event. I know there will be one final event as the sun of my life moves toward the western horizon where the transition from physical earthly life to eternal life occurs as death meets eternity. And God is in and through every aspect of the transition. Then I move into an eternal experience that a loving God has promised and I do not need to know just what that is like. A wonderful new life begins that never ends!

September 16, 2017

Ample Power to Meet Whatever Comes

> *May you be strengthened with all power, according to his glorious might, for all endurance and patience with joy, giving thanks to the Father, who has qualified us to share in the inheritance of the saints in light.*
> — Col. 1:11

Looking back over ninety-six years of life I can see more clearly how God's good hand of loving providence has shaped my journey. Along the way I was often uncertain about my choices as I sought to find the will of God as I stood at various crossroads. Then I chose with faith, but now I feel confirmed that it was God's grace that blessed my life. Now I look away from the long and rich days of the past and I look forward to the short days of the future. Now I pray that I will be strengthened by God's power to meet whatever comes with endurance and patience, and a depth of joy as I am filled with gratitude to God.

So many of my loved ones have quietly passed through the end of earthly life out of the valley of shadows into the brilliant life of eternity where the struggles and sufferings of earthly life are no more, but joy, love and peace fill our never-ending days. I trust God.

November 27, 2017

The Absent God and the Present God

Behold, I go forward, but he is not there;
And backward, but I cannot perceive him;
On his left hand, I seek him, but I cannot behold him;
I turn to the right hand, but I cannot see him
JOB 23:8–9

But he knows the way that I take;
When he has tried me I shall come forth as gold.
JOB 23:10

BY LANCELOT ANDREWS (1555–1626)*

Lord, be within me to strengthen me;
    Without me to keep me;
    Above me to protect me;
    Beneath me to uphold me;
    Before me to direct me;
    Behind me to keep me from straying;
    Round about me to defend me.

*In *Prayers Ancient and Modern*, page 264.

Part 10

Christmas

Bethlehem

Bethlehem Christmas carols.
O Little Town of Bethlehem,
How still we see thee lie!
Above thy deep and dreamless sleep
The silent stars go by.
Yet in thy dark streets shineth
The everlasting light;
The hopes and fears of all the years
Are met in thee tonight.

O come, all ye faithful,
Joyful and triumphant,
O come ye,
O come ye to Bethlehem.
O come let us adore Him,
O come let us adore Him,
Christ the Lord.

Now! Come with me to Bethlehem.
Bethlehem from ancient times
Is marked the place
Where Jesus was born.
We enter the manger square.
There stands the church of the Nativity.
Israeli soldiers with guns on their shoulders
Stand and walk about with eyes alert.
To enter the Church we must
Bow our heads and stoop down.

The entrance is purposefully low
So that anyone entering, must bow their heads
As a symbol of humility.
As we approach the sacred place.
Entering we see bulbs of blue, red, and yellow
Hanging from the ceiling.
All is quiet and still.
To the right of the altar is a doorway.
It leads to a circular stairway going down
To a cave, that is not large.
The base of the cave is natural stone.
The spot where Jesus was born
Is roped off where visitors
Can look but not go.
A Baptist minister in his deep devotion
Steps over the rope and
Kneels on the stone and prays.
On a nearby bench three nuns sit
With their dresses of black and white,
And now and then softly
Hum a tune, Silent Night, Holy night.
Some ancient Christian scholars believe
Jesus was born in a cave.

This special moment is filled with meaning
In the still and quiet reverence,
As we ponder the mystery of Jesus' birth
As did Mary do long ago.
This may be the very place
Where God became incarnate in human flesh.
Thinking about the mystery of this reality
Something deep is reached in the human spirit.

And now in this present moment of quietness
We close our eyes and ponder just
What Jesus' birth means,
The mystery of God incarnate in human flesh
And we worship!

Slowly and silently with reverence
We ascend the stairs
With hearts filled with awe and wonder.
Leaving the Church of the Nativity
We bow and stoop again
With a deepened humility,
And go out into the Manger Square
Where the Israeli soldiers
With guns and eyes alert
Walk to and fro.
And as we look at the starry sky above
    We sing:

O come, all ye faithful
Joyful and triumphant.
O come ye, O come to Bethlehem.
Come and behold him
Born the king of angels.
O come let us adore him,
O come let us adore him,
O come let us adore him,
Christ the Lord!

December 1, 2013

The Savior's Birth

May the star which led
The wise men to the Christ child
Lead you to the worship
Of Christ the Lord.

May the angels that announced
The Savior's birth
To the humble shepherds
Announce again the good news to you.

May the animals in the stable
In all of their lowly estate
Remind you to be humble before
The King of Kings and Lord of Lords.

Christmas 2005

Christmas Silence

Santa Claus jingles,
Church bells ringing,
Choirs singing,
Children laughing,
Wonderful sounds of Christmas.

Beyond the sounds is silence.
Quiet, still, gentle silence.
Listen! Hear the silence.
How silently, how silently
The wondrous gift is given.

Christmas 2004

A Christmas Poem for a Violent World

The Gospel of John says that Jesus is the light of the world.
The light of the world shines in the darkness
And the darkness has not put it out . . . AND IT NEVER WILL!!

When Jesus was born in Bethlehem
The world was not a safe place.
Herod ordered his soldiers
To kill every male child in Bethlehem
Two years old and under.
Hebrew mothers were distraught and weeping.
If you visited the Vatican
You would see several tapestries depicting
Herod's slaying the children of Bethlehem.
Joseph dreamed a dream in which an angel
Told him to take the baby Jesus and his mother to Egypt.
So by God's providence Jesus was saved from the massacre.

Jesus finished his mission on earth
As he suffered the agony of the cruel cross.

Today our world is not a safe place.
In Syria women and children under two years of age
Are killed along with boys and men.
In Iraq Isis soldiers cut off the heads of Christians and others,
Creating an unimaginable horror scene.
In America, random shooters kill

In children's schools, movie theaters,
And even in church where people
Have gone to pray.

Today the resurrected and living Jesus
Is in the world of violence.
He is in hundreds of places
And in the hearts of thousands of people.
Through the violent centuries
People of faith have found Jesus.
They do not understand the violence.
They wonder why a loving God
Does not intervene!

It may be that the Prince of Peace
Suffers along with us and his presence
Assures us that all the Herods of the world,
And makers and users of crosses
and other weapons of death,
Will not silence the Prince of Peace
Who puts the dreams of Peace
In human hearts that keeps hope alive.

A Relevant Comment
There are stories from World War I, which was basically a trench war. At Christmas, when the allied soldiers would sing "Silent Night, Holy Night," the German soldiers would sing "Stille Nacht, Heilige Nacht." Such is the power of Christmas that its song would rise above the war being fought. Christmas came in spite of the violent war. Even today, even now when we sing "Silent Night" it brings the reality of God's incarnation in spite

of the violence all around us. Let us be aware of this as we sing "Silent Night."

May you be blessed by the assurance that Christmas brings,
That God has become incarnate in Jesus Christ and is with us in these violent and uncertain times.

Prayer: Eternal God, give us courage and hope, knowing
That in these dark times Jesus is the light of the world and
The darkness has not put it out, AND IT NEVER WILL!!

Christmas 2017

Christmas 2016

Christmas 2016 looks like the whole world is ablaze—violence, suffering on a large scale, changes, fear and uncertainty. It is true here in America also. Surely each of us has thought a lot about the situation and has had varied and conflicted feelings about what is happening. Today I want what I say to have some relevance to what is happening.

To begin I want to recognize that Christmas is about the incarnation of God in Jesus Christ. Paul said "Great is the mystery of our religion." The mystery of our religion began when Jesus was born of a virgin in Bethlehem, with angels singing and announcing the good news. The mystery of our religion was also at the end of Jesus' earthly life when he was resurrected which gives us the hope of eternal life.

In between Jesus' birth and resurrection Jesus showed us and taught us what God does on earth. He healed the sick, opened the eyes of the blind, caused the lame to walk, forgave sins. He loved mankind, taught us to love one another, taught us what is the heart of our religion: to love God with our heart, mind, soul, and strength, and to love our neighbor as ourselves. Jesus showed us the depth of God's love when he endured the agony of the cross. By what he did and taught he made it clear that the eternal God is in our lives and in the world.

We do not always know what God will do or when God will act in us or our world. But the faith of our religion, and especially the faith of our Presbyterian religion, strongly believes in the providence of God and that the eternal and sovereign God is in our lives and in the world, and that there are times when we have done all we can, when we must leave what happens in the hands of God.

In World War II the world faced the raw evil of Hitler and it was at that time that so many faced the cruelty and death of war. There were times when we were not sure just how it would turn out. It was at that time that John Southerland Bonnell, the distinguished minister of the Fifth Ave. Presbyterian Church in New York, told the amazing story about when to leave things in the hand of God. I think it has some relevance to the times in which we are living:

WHEN TO LEAVE EVENTS IN THE HAND OF GOD

"On the night of July 10, 1943, a vast army of three thousand ships containing eighty thousand Allied soldiers sailed across the waters from Malta to the shores of Sicily in a great amphibious operation. General Eisenhower, surrounded by his staff officers, stood on a high hill overlooking the Malta harbor. In the light of a full moon shining down on the sea he watched the troop-laden ships weigh anchor and sail out into the mists while squadrons of planes roared into the sky. Deeply moved, Eisenhower sprang to attention and saluted his heroic men. Then he bowed his head in silent prayer, his staff joining him in this brief act of devotion. Turning to an officer beside him, Eisenhower said: 'There comes a time when you've used your brains, your training, your technical skill, and the die is cast and the events are in the hands of God, and there you have to leave them.'"

December 1, 2016

Part 11

Peace

Put Your Touches on My Spirit, O Lord

Put your touches on my spirit, O Lord.
There are times when my spirit sags.
There is a certain heaviness,
And a general weariness.
The glow is dim and sometimes flickers.

At times like these I yearn for your touch.
Yours is the perfect gentleness.
Gently touch my spirit with renewed faith,
And brighten my window of hope,
And warm my heart with love.

At times like these
Let me lie down for a while
In your green pastures,
And let me walk by the quiet and still waters,
Until my spirit is restored.

August 27, 2009

The Master's Touch

By Richard E. Byrd*

April 14, 1934

. . . Took my daily walk at 4:00 pm today, in 89 degrees of frost. The sun had dropped below the horizon, and a blue—of a richness I've never seen anywhere else—flooded in, extinguishing all but the dying embers of the sunset.

Due west, halfway to the zenith, Venus was an unblinking diamond; and opposite her, in the eastern sky, was a brilliant twinkling star set off exquisitely, as was Venus, in the sea of blue. In the northeast a silver-green serpentine aurora pulsed and quivered gently. In places the Barrier's whiteness had the appearance of dull platinum. It was all delicate and illusive. The colors were subdued and not numerous; the jewels few; the setting simple. But the way these things went together showed a master's touch.

I paused to listen to the silence. My breath, crystallized as it passed by my cheeks, drifted on a breeze gentler than a whisper. The wind vane pointed toward the South Pole. Presently the wind cups ceased their gentle turning as the cold killed the breeze. My frozen breath hung like a cloud overhead.

The day was dying, the night being born—but with great peace. Here were the imponderable processes and forces of the cosmos, harmonious and soundless. Harmony, that was it! That was what came out of the silence—a gentle rhythm, the strain of a perfect chord, the music of the spheres, perhaps.

It was enough to catch that rhythm, momentarily to be myself a part of it. In that instant I could feel no doubt of man's oneness with the universe. The conviction came that that rhythm was too orderly, too harmonious, too perfect to be a product of blind chance—that, therefore, there must be purpose in the accidental offshoot. It was a feeling that transcended reason; that went to the heart of man's despair and found it groundless. The universe was a cosmos, not a chaos; man was as rightfully a part of that cosmos as were the day and night.

*From *Alone: The Classic Polar Adventure*, page 63, 645.

Part 12

Death and Eternal Life

The Basic Fear

By Paul Tillich*

For fear is, above all, fear of the unknown; and the darkness of the unknown is filled with the images created by fear. This is true even with respect to events on the plane of daily life: The unknown face terrifies the infant; the unknown will of the parent and the teacher creates fear in the child; and all the unknown implications of any situation or new task produce fear, which is the feeling of not being able to handle the situation. All this is true to an absolute degree with respect to death—the absolutely unknown; the darkness in which there is no light at all, and in which even imagination vanishes; that darkness in which all acting and controlling cease, and in which everything which we were is finished; the most necessary and impossible idea at the same time; the real and ultimate object of fear from which all other fears derive their power, that fear that overwhelmed even Christ at Gethsemane.

*From "*The Shaking of the Foundations*," page 170.

Death

By Tennessee Williams*

BIG MAMA: Time goes by so fast. Nothin' can outrun it. Death commences too early—almost before you're half-acquainted with life—you meet with the other . . . oh, you know we just got to love each other and stay together, all of us, just as close as we can, especially now that such a black thing has come and moved into this place without invitation.

*From "Cat on a Hot Tin Roof," in *Best American Plays* (1951–57 ed.), page 76.

Listen to the Easter Lily

Thoughts stirred by a poem by Mary Mckee Snell

Beneath the cover of the sod
The lily bulb heard the call of God.
In the mystery of God
The answering pulse began to beat.
The sod lay damp, dark and cold.
But never did the lily ask,
Who shall roll the stone away?
But it came forth to bloom
And show forth the beauty of life.

So our souls do not cling to the earth,
But they hear God's call to new birth.
The cover lid of the soil of death
Cannot keep the soul
From responding to the call of God.
Breaking through the sod of death,
The soul emerges into a beautiful
And fuller life and rejoices
To find itself with God.

August 4, 2014

The Presence of a Loved One

Here are two poems that might be material for the Easter season. We talk about the presence of God and many devotional materials tell us how we may feel God's presence. We also talk about our departed loved one being with God, saying "He or she is with God." God is spirit, and if we believe our loved ones have eternal life, then is it not reasonable to believe that since they are present with God, and we feel God's presence, then we can also feel the presence of our loved ones? Of course this has to do with spirit and nothing visible. We remember our loved ones and may even be aware of them in a special way. But what I am talking about is a bit deeper than remembrance and imagination. I realize I am dealing with the great mystery of life and death, and I do not want to imply that I know anything more than others in this area. I was interested when I linked the presence of God and the possible presence of a loved one.

I have not seen any theological writing that connects God's presence with the presence of our loved ones. Of course, we do not know just how everything will be, and I certainly do not claim to have any special wisdom or insight. I advance the idea that since God in spirit has a presence, and our loved one continues with eternal life and they are with God, then it may be that they too can have a presence. If this is true, then many people may be comforted by feeling that maybe they can have a sense of their loved ones' presence.

February 22, 2018

Reflections from the Reality of God's Presence

In the ancient deep darkness humans
did not know they were made in the image of God.
They cried out with Job: If a man die, can he live again?
At the end he said: I had heard of thee
by the hearing of the ear, but now my eye sees thee.
Job died an old man and full of days.
This is the foundation of the beginning of an
authentic relationship with God.

In my experience I have felt connected
to the sovereign God. Connected to God's power
and to God's strong love. As I have read the
stories of Jesus I have a clearer picture
of what God is like. His words of life, hope,
and promise have given me assurance,
and my spirit and soul are at peace.
Through the centuries faithful Christians
Have affirmed that "in life and death
We are with God."

This is where I am at the age of ninety-six years.

December 13, 2017

Reflections from Age Ninety-Six

The separation when death comes is a loss of the total being.
We long for their touch, their smile, their laughter.
These are things that are lost from the body.
Our loved one is gone. It is real and it is hard!

We use our reason as did C. S. Lewis when his wife died.
He was talking about the state of his wife as pure intellect.
Then he thought of the concept of the resurrection of the body
And added: "We cannot understand. The best is perhaps
what we understand least." We reach out with faith
and look for answers that will give us strength.

Then, just maybe something emerges that seems valid.
Our loved one is with God, and God is with us.
We are both being held in God's love.
If it is possible to feel God's presence,
would it not be reasonable to feel the presence of our loved one?
Jesus said, "Because I live you too shall live."
Our being alive with eternal life would mean
that we could have presence of soul and spirit,
not the physical and fleshy body.

With this thought by reason, and with faith,
as both reason and faith are joined together,
we may have a valid experience of the presence of our loved ones.
We can remember our loved ones, but this concept
of their presence goes deeper than remembrance.

With this in mind, on a recent night I had a deep sense
that my wife and son were here with me.
When my father died I would often walk out alone under the stars
and be comforted by the feeling that
though my father had gone, my heavenly
Father would never leave me.

Now the idea of presence will help me
to see that in addition to feeling the presence of God,
I can be comforted that I can
feel the presence of my loved ones.

December 14, 2017

God's Other Room

By Albert S. Coats

'Tis passing strange how nearer seems a friend
Whose home has been far distant from your own,
When you have learned that he has passed within
The mystic shrine denied as yet to us,
And sacred kept for those found worthy death.
Now, now, you say, I have him safe and near
As God is near to all who hold Him true.

But yesterday I learned that one whose face
Was beautiful in glowing womanhood
When first I knew her, two score years away,
And ever grew more beautiful, as soul
Took on new beauty in its homeward growth,
Had gained her entrance into life indeed.
Now seems she not a thousand miles away
But very near in the adjoining room!
As full of kindly interest as before,
With added powers for strength and comforting.

Nor do I have to seek me wizard test
To know she is alive and very near,
Since she's with God and God is here and now!
Nor will I rudely try to lift the latch.
'Tis God shall whisper: "Now the feast is spread,
And you may come! Full welcome to the board!"
So will I think of loving friends who now
Are living safely in God's other room.

There Is a Life to Come

Make me unafraid as I follow
the way of life for all who
have lived on this earth.
I give thanks for the miracle
of resurrection. I call to mind
the word of the Scottish theologian*:

"If God is justice and God is love,
I am as certain as it is possible
to be certain of anything that
there is a life to come."

March 24, 2018

*Dr. William Barclay

A Little Strip of Sea

How far away is the Beyond?
With the last heartbeat
It is just a little strip of sea
And the Beyond is there!
Strange new place? Not exactly!
For a new Garden of Eden
Is peopled with saints and prophets,
Who lived on earth
Long before I saw the light of day,
And loved ones who are newcomers!
They emerge from the new Eden
Where everything (there is no thing)
Is perfectly suited for Souls and Spirits.
There is nothing needed for
Bodies of flesh and bone and blood.
For old things of the earth
Have passed away and are replaced
By a new and wonderful eternity
Where there is indescribable
Peace and joy and all yearnings
Of the spirit are realized.
And a wonderful surprise!
We "fit in" totally to this new life,
And we are at home—to stay.

May 4, 2014

The Transition

Three days before Easter

Everybody dies!
We have known that from our earliest years.
But for a lifetime it seems far off.
Then as we move through our seventies
Death is dimly seen in the gloom of the distant future.
In the eighties and nineties it becomes
Clearer and more focused.
Of course death can come at any time,
But now we know it is not far off.

We have been living on solid earth
And witnessed the seasons as they come and go.
We have experienced happiness and joy
And we have struggled with
Problems and hurts that are real.
We have experienced the ups and downs of living.

When death comes it is as if a television
That has been showing pictures
And telling stories of vibrant human life,
And the off switch is pushed,
And all is quiet and still.
No pictures, no music, no voice.

A Scottish minister and theologian
On the edge of dying after a declining illness said:

"I am looking forward to seeing
What it is like on the other side of death."
Others are filled with fear of the unknown.
Over the centuries unnumbered
People who with the warm light of faith
And the quiet confidence of trust
In the good God of mercy and love,
Move into a new life that has no ending.

Thanks be to God for the reality
Of the resurrection of Jesus Christ who said:
"Because I live you shall live also."

April 21, 2011

The Growing Spirit

It is the nature of living things to grow.
Seed produces its likeness.
Acorns become oak trees
Flowers produce blossoms.
Animals grow into adult animals.
Human babies grow into adult men and women.

But can growth go on and on?
An oak tree may live a hundred years or more.
But it dies.
Flowers flourish and bloom
But they wither and fade away.
Animals grow into adults of their species,
But ultimately they age and die.
So with humans.
They grow in body, mind, and spirit,
But eventually die; no exceptions.

The body dies, the mind ceases to be.
The spirit? It may still live!
Could it be that the spirit
Grows on throughout eternity?
Mystery!

October 11, 2009

A Sparkling Moment

Now and then there is a sparkling moment.

Times Past flashes on my memory.
The good times. The special times.
Childhood experiences.
Adolescence and awareness years.
Special people.
Dreams unforgettable.

Times Present. Gratitude for the past.
Gratitude for the present.
Warm and happy experiences.
Loved ones that care.
Friends that are there.

Times to come. Faith that brings hope.
Love that generates security.
Reflections on past mercies
That are a pledge of future grace.

A glimpse of the wholeness of life.
God was there at the beginning.
God is here now.
God will be there at the end.

Thanks be to God for
His love that is from everlasting to everlasting.

February 5, 2006

Deep Calm

The sea ebbs and flows with waves large and small.
The fury of wind and storm
Agitate only the surface of the sea.
They may penetrate two or three hundred feet,
But below that is the calm and unruffled deep.

Life goes on from day to day
Like restless waves out at sea
And their gentle lapping on the shore.
But there are days when the strong winds blow
And occasionally with the fury of a storm.
Then we are troubled, agitated and anxious.
We are ruffled and disturbed and maybe scared.

The human spirit has the capacity for great depth.
When at our deepest level there is a strong faith
In the eternal God of love,
It brings a deep sense of calmness
That gives us stability,
When the strong and stormy winds
That come to all on life's journey
Disturb and test our spirits.

July 11, 2008

Spirit to Spirit

> *The important thing is to know our purpose in entering the inner world, and to know that we are looking for the Risen Christ and a relationship with Him.*
>
> — Morton T. Kelsey*

We are more than a physical body.
There is a wonderful intangible
That is the soul or spirit or psyche.
It is mysteriously interwoven with the body,
But when the body becomes still and lifeless
This intangible continues to be.

The Word became incarnate in human flesh.
God's intangible Spirit became interwoven with the body.
When the body of Jesus was crucified
It became still and lifeless.
God in Jesus did not cease to be.
But in the mystery beyond comprehension and understanding
It manifested itself again in the Risen Christ.

As we in our living bodies reach beyond them
To the intangible part of us
Which is soul, spirit, or psyche.
We probe in the world of spirit,
And that is the world of the Risen Christ.
There with spirit to spirit

A spiritual relationship can occur.
When it does and the relationship grows,
We then experience the transforming
Power of the spirit of Christ.
Living in that relationship we experience
Deep and significant changes taking place in us.
And bit by bit a new, stronger, and better person emerges.

July 27, 2006

*In *The Other Side of Silence*, page 140.

I Have Lost Myself

Betty Pope Scott Noble
Died August 7, 2012

"I feel like I have lost myself."

She had always been full of life.
She was always active and happy,
Filled with unselfishness and love,
Her wonderful spirit
Touching all who were around her.

Now something was changing.
She was confused and afraid.
She felt alone as clouds and shadows
Closed around her. She wondered:
"What is happening to me?
Don't leave me!"
What had always been clear and bright
Was slipping away.
The dark unknown was engulfing her.
I do not know just what
It is like to lose yourself.
But she was hurt and disturbed
As she felt who she was
Was getting away from her.

We surrounded her with strong love
As we were suffering with her.
In her fear she asked:
"Are you going to take care of me?"
With heavy hearts she was assured
Time and time again.

It took several years for her
Indomitable spirit to be destroyed,
And it never was completely overcome.
But it took some time for the final
Curtains to be closed.

When they were closed
We suffered with the reality
That she was gone.
As we looked through the darkness
To the far horizon.
We yearned for the sun to rise
And shine its light on us
And our diminished world.

July 15, 2014

Assurance of Grace

By Ron Wallace

Blessings
Occur.

Some days I find myself
putting my foot in
the same stream twice;
leading a horse to water
and making him drink.
I have a clue.
I can see the forest
for the trees.

All around me people
are making silk purses
out of sows' ears,
getting blood from turnips,
building Rome in a day.
There's a business
like show business.
There's something new
under the sun.

Some days misery
no longer loves company;
it puts itself out of its.
There's rest for the weary.

There's turning back.
There are guarantees.
I can be serious.
I can mean that.
You can quite
put your finger on it.

Some days I know
I am long for this world.
I can go home again.
And when I go
I can take it with me.

Part 13

Mystery

Mystery

At the outer edge of all human knowledge
There is the vast mystery
Of the unknown and maybe eternally unknowable.

We are able to know the planet
On which we live—our knowing
Is the matter, the substance we see and feel,
And the intangibles we experience in many ways.
Mankind's deep research enables us
To understand much about our planet,
And our life upon it, as it
Leisurely spins in surrounding space.

Then there are the sun, moon, and stars.
We have reached the moon
And solved some of its mysteries.
We may reach other planets
And solve some of their mysteries.
But way beyond the moon and sun
There are visible stars.
And beyond the stars
And how they got there
Is the wholly unknown.
Its name is mystery.
Where did "what is" come from?
Was there once nothing—absolutely nothing?

We have been informed and enlightened
By scientists, astronomers, physicists, mathematicians,
Psychologists, philosophers, theologians, and visionaries.
All have pushed back, way back
The boundaries where knowledge and mystery meet.
But the wonderfully expanded boundaries
Of knowledge leave the vastness
Which has none other name than: mystery.

As the human mind searches and explores
And hungers for more knowledge
Of the ultimate unknown called mystery,
There may be only one authentic stance:
Vast humility with a drop of faith.

May 23, 2006

The God-given Sense of Right and Wrong

Thoughts stimulated by Ecclesiastes 3:11 and a quotation from Kant's Critique of Practical Reason, *published in 1788:*
"The starry heavens above me and the moral law within me."

God has put eternity in the heart
That sets the human being
Apart from all God's creation.
That eternity is recognized
In the moral sense of right and wrong.
It is a seed that is mysteriously
Planted in the heart of every child.
We see it when a child cries out:
"That is not fair!"
The nature of any seed planted in the ground is to grow,
And also it is the nature of the seed
Planted in the human heart to grow.
Without certain conditions some seed does not grow,
Or they produce a small and immature plant.

Each time the moral sense of right and wrong
Is recognized in the human spirit
And is obeyed, then the moral sense
Grows and becomes clearer and stronger,
And produces a good moral character.
Also each time that moral sense is disobeyed,
It tends to shrivel in the soul
And result in a weak moral character.

August 29, 2009

Prayer and Mystery

By William Adams Brown*

Eternal Father, whom the heaven
And earth cannot contain . . .
There is so much life
That we cannot understand,
So much that it is hard to bear.
We come into Thy Presence
Seeking at Thy call
To press through the shadows.
We are compassed about with mystery,
The mystery of life,
And the mystery of death,
The mystery of love,
And the mystery of hate,
The mystery of sin,
And the mystery of the Cross
That atones for sin.
O Thou who art Thyself
The mystery of mysteries
And at the same time
Light of light,
Part the clouds that hide Thy face
And reveal Thyself unto us today.

September 14, 2014

*Abridged prayer in *Five Minutes a Day*, by Robert E. Speer, page 363.

Great Is the Mystery of God

Great is the mystery of God.
The mystery is because God
Is more than we can imagine.
We believe in God,
But like the ancient Greeks
A God is not fully known.

As Paul said, the unknown God
We worship is now revealed to us
In Jesus Christ.
There we know more about who God is.
Though far beyond our human knowledge,
In Jesus we know that God
Is the God of love.

August 20, 2014

On the Edge of Mystery

There was a deep stirring in my soul
    this morning.

I did not want anything to intrude.
No telephone, no sound of television
Or radio. Not even the sound of music.
The still quietness engulfed me.
The mystery of the soul,
The mystery of what is beyond.
A deeper penetration of the mystery
    of human life.

I felt as if eternity
And the present time were meeting.
Spirit, my spirit, God's spirit
Were mingled in the present moment.
The essence of the mystery of it all
Seemed to be tantalizing.
A glimpse of a new reality
And then the fading into
The cloud of mystery.

What is happening?
A new and deeper awareness
Of the mystery and wonder of life.

May 25, 2013

Part 14

Character

A Parable

For Betty Scott Noble

She was going about her purpose-driven life.
She loved children and with her knowledge and skill
Helped them with their early struggles of growing up.

There was a knock at the door.
When she opened the door
There stood the ugliest and most vicious-
Looking creature with glaring eyes
And a threatening scowl.
His name was cancer.
She fought him with the use
Of the best scientific and medical skills
And with steady faith and hope.
And he was gone.

As she continued her purpose-driven life
Of loving and helping children,
There was another knock at the door.
She opened the door
And there stood the same ugly
And vicious-looking creature.
Again she ran him off with
Scientific and medical tools,
And with her strong and steady faith and hope.

She went back to her purpose-driven life
Of loving and helping children.
In time there was another knock at the door.
There stood the same ugly
And threatening being as before.
Again she bravely fought
With the best scientific and medical tools.
And he was gone.

Many years later there was another knock on the door.
She opened the door with fear and trembling
And there stood a loving Jesus with open arms.

November 15, 2014

Three Metals

You are as scrap iron,
And it shows one quality of your life:
A spirit that is strong, tough, and rugged.

You are also as silver,
Sterling silver.
Your character is sterling as
Honesty and integrity are at the core of your life.
You are authentic,
With no pretense or falseness.

You are also as gold,
Pure gold.
As you have gone through the fire,
The dross has been burned away
And there remains a quality of being
That only can be described as pure gold.

Scrap iron, sterling silver, pure gold.

December 12, 2009

My daughter, Betty Scott Noble, was blessed by a strong Noble and Scott heritage.

Part 15

General

The Church Upon The Rock Was Built

SANCTA CIVITAS 8686 86   HERBERT HOWELLS

1. The Church up-on the Rock was built and through the Cent-uries lives. We thrive with-in its fel-low-ship and Wor-ship God here-in.
2. This Church up-on this place has been through earthquake and fire has stood. With joy in all for which it stands and con-fi-dence for good.
3. This Church-'s past is true and strong through faith of form-er Saints. We move a-long to-geth-- er and give to God our thanks.
4. This Church be-yond its past does look and through the coming years will serve. We thrill to see its pre-sent faith and from its life draw strength.

Im-bue us with your grace and pow'r to serve with faith and cour-age.

Text written by Dr. J. Phillips Noble upon the 250th anniversary celebration of First (Scots) Presbyterian Church, November 8, 1981.

The Church Upon the Rock Was Built

The Church upon the Rock was built
And through the centuries lives.
We thrive within its fellowship
And worship God herein.
      Refrain: Imbue us with your grace and pow'r
      To serve with faith and courage.

This Church upon this place has been through
Earthquake and fire and has stood
With joy in all for which it stands
And confidence for good.
      Refrain: Imbue us with your grace and pow'r
      To serve with faith and courage.

This Church, its past is true and strong
Through faith of former saints.
We move along together
And give to God our thanks.
      Refrain: Imbue us with your grace and pow'r
      To serve with faith and courage.

This Church beyond its past does look
And through the coming years will serve.
We thrill to see its present faith
And from its life draw strength.
      Refrain: Imbue us with your grace and pow'r
      To serve with faith and courage.

November 8, 1981

The Limits of Responsibility

> "The responsibility of a father or a government leader is limited by the responsibility of the child or the citizen."
> — Dietrich Bonhoeffer*

Many parents worry about their children.
They often feel the weight of the responsibility for their children,
and parents do have a responsibility,
but there is a limit to this responsibility.

In some Christian churches a child is brought for Baptism.
Part of the meaning of this is that the child is
recognized as a child of God.
Parents enter into a covenant with God
to teach the child of God's love for them.
As the child grows up there are three
who have a responsibility: God, the parents, and the child.

God will be faithful in God's responsibility.
The parents can feel that they and God are
involved in the raising of their children,
and that they are not alone.

But there is a limit to what the parents can do.
As the child grows he or she has
some responsibility for themselves.

The responsibility of the parents is huge,
but at some point what the parent can do
is limited, and the child is responsible for the
life choices that are made.
They are then left in the hands of God.

August 25, 2016

*From A Year of Devotions, page 238.

A Poem

By Wendell Berry*

Great deathly powers have passed:
The black and bitter cold, the wind
That broke and felled strong trees, the rind
Of ice that held at last.

Even the fleshly heart
In cold that made it seem a stone.
And now there comes again the one
First Sabbath light, the Art

That unruled, uninvoked,
Unknown, makes new again and heals,
Restores heart's flesh so that it feels
Anew the old deadlocked

Goodness of its true home
That it will lose again and mourn,
Remembering the year reborn
In almost perfect bloom

In almost shadeless wood,
Sweet air that neither burned nor chilled
In which the tenderest flowers prevailed,
The light made flesh and blood.

*From Randy Calvo, a poem that touched him.

The Communion of Family and Friends

So many in the family have gone.
Also many others who were in my world
    Have gone.
        It is often a bit lonely.

But there are times when
The presence of God is felt.
And being surrounded
By the communion of saints
Means the heavenly company
Of family and friends
And many others,
Some from a long time ago,
Are there as a great
Company of people.
The bond of love of family and friends
Is still there and our Minds,
Hearts and Spirits are warmed
As we think of them.

February 24, 2014

Darkness and a Tiny Point of Light

By Patricia Boinest Potter*

I sit with pillows piled high on my lap
My pad resting on top
Aligned with a picture high on my shelf
Of my father holding my tiny self
High in the air.

Seeing the earth curve into the distance
As time moves and curves in its wholeness.
I can see only a portion of this map.
It is Umberto Eco's 1:1 map with a twist
Like the Mobius.
It can turn inside out.
It is a (s)trip that ends where it started
Where the whole ocean meets a grain of sand.

Perhaps I am like the migrating starling
Moving outside of the flock.
The map of this movement of T. S. Eliot's turning point.
I am the vanishing point.

Morels are with butter in the pan.
Grown in the wild
They connect ismorphically with
The spirit of the wild salmon.
Their map accompanies us
On our journey.

I draw lines tracing our movement.
They disappear into the darkness.
Pencil lines are fragile
They can be erased so easily,
By a touch.

Spirit, my father's spirit, my same otherness
Sometimes seems to disappear . . .
But it is still here.

The sky, the dark.
The blackest I have ever seen
No stars. No moon.
No shadowy shapes of trees.

Dark ground. Dark, dark.
I seek to map the darkness.
But first it must become a part.
It is drawn through by an unknowing
Pattern deep within.

Within the darkest dark of the pattern is a tiny point of light.

I can't extinguish it.

A tiny light
Hiding deep
Deep within.

It is like a new thought.
I can't tell you if it is mine or if it is a part of the dark.
The deeper I go the tiny light calls to me.

I try to blow it out.

I want to map the darkness.

At the end of the Darkness
Is a mirror.
I finally see and know . . .
I am that tiny light.

Suddenly I see
It is a two-way mirror.
My father is there.
Am I reflecting his light?
Or is it my own?
Or are they the same?

March 7, 2015

*My artist friend, whose father died when she was twelve years old.

Two Consciences

"There is a warning conscience
And a gnawing conscience.
The warning conscience comes before sin.
The gnawing conscience follows after sin."*

The conscience is hard to describe,
But everybody "knows" what it is.
We are born with it.
"God has put eternity into man's mind.**
"Two things fill the mind with ever increasing awe:
The starry heavens above me,
And the moral law within me."***

We are familiar with warning signs on the highways.
There are also warning signs on the highway of life.
To ignore the warning signs is risky.
The conscience erects warning signs
On the highway of life.
The conscience which will not go away
Nags at us when the warning signs are ignored.

November 3, 2010

---

*A Diary Of Reading, by John Baillie, page 289.
**Ecclesiastes 3:11.
***Immanuel Kant, *Critique of Practical Reason* quoted in "*The Intellectual Devotion*," Kidder and Oppenheim, page 237

Yearning

After ten years of ministry in the First Presbyterian Church in Anniston, Alabama, the Jespersons and the Turners, elders in the church, made it possible for me to go to New College in Edinburgh, Scotland, for a term of study. They also made it possible for my wife Betty to join me after the term was over for a grand tour of Europe. Mr. Turner, who had traveled many times to Europe and loved it very much, said to me as he contemplated my going to Europe, "Phil, I would give anything if I could see the coastline of Europe for the first time again." He had seen it from aboard a ship as it gradually came into view and the thrill for him was unforgettable.

Old People Can Grow

Reflections from age ninety

My body had its day!
There is still something there,
But not much.

My mind still functions,
But it is not hitting on all cylinders.
What is left moves slowly.
Much of the past is really past!
Much of the present does not stay long.

With my soul/spirit it is different.
In it is plenty of room for growth.
Love can become warmer.
Joy can increase.
Peace can deepen.
Then there is patience.
Sometimes there seems to be more impatience
Than patience, so I am told!
Here is a place to grow.

And kindness! Unkindness sometimes
Raises its unwanted head.
I can train my spirit to be kinder.

Goodness. When people ask, "How are you?"
The apostle Paul and the great reformer
John Calvin say, I cannot answer I am good.
But we say, I may not be good
But I am working on it.

And there is faithfulness.
If I have been known to break faith,
My spirit can grow to be more faithful.

Gentleness. The hymn says:
Thou hast the perfect gentleness.
That is God, Not me.
But careful attention to my spirit
Can increase my gentleness.

Ah! The last one is self-control.
The term itself says whose responsibility that is.
The control levers are in my spirit.
We can grow our spirit
To learn how to use them.

So, my body and mind
May be beyond much further growth.
But my spirit/soul
May be at its best time to grow.

March 23, 2011

Postscript

Dr. Rick Reed is a member of the First Scots Presbyterian Church in Charleston, S.C., where I was the minister from 1972 to 1982. When I heard he had pancreatic cancer and had only a few months to live, I wrote him a letter and enclosed two books of poetry and quotations that I had written. I received the following remarkable response about the compatibility of science and religion. In his words, "I have spent a lot of time exploring all the questions and mysteries of which you speak and have enclosed my own thoughts on science and religion being compatible. New discoveries have brought me closer to God rather than allowing scientific laws to replace God." His response is reprinted here with his permission

Reflections on Phil Noble's "Words That Stretch the Mind and Lift the Spirit"

God, Science, and Religion

As life becomes more fragile, it is natural to reflect upon what has gone on before, what importance has been gleaned, and where do we go from here. The Before of my life was filled with mistakes and sin. However, from this human frailty many truths have emerged, while much remains unresolved. Facing terminal pancreatic cancer encourages a revisit to an unresolved before and after life perspective.

We have been assured that the incomplete will be revealed when the promise of a "life after death" is fulfilled through our trust and faith in all the forms the Creator manifests (Christ central). Thus I have no sense of desperation, but view my reflections, in common with Phil Noble, as a means to share with others who may wish to engage their own search. Phil helps bring this all into perspective and strengthens our faith in what is seen and what is unseen.

In Phil's earlier book, *Words and Images That Seep into the Soul*, we receive lessons for life that prepare us to engage the lingering questions that are in his new collection of poems. Faith, trust, love, and continued growth are affirmed, but many *mysteries* remain unresolved. Phil emphasizes that not being able to understand all the magnitudes of God is not a stumbling block, but an encouragement to continue searching for God through Jesus Christ. Acting upon God's word in behalf of others draws us closer in this search. This passion for love of fellowman must continue until death.

A. ALTHOUGH DARKNESS IS very real for Phil, his emphasis on light is timely. Light in many ways must be connected to the essence of God:

1) Energy abounds in the Universe and by $E=MC^2$ we can imagine, perhaps understand, an origin of creation and ongoing life, death, and "resurrection," as one form converts to the other.

2) Although light is just one form of electromagnetic waves, it is the most observable of forms. It is frequently emitted when quantum mechanics are expressed. Gravitational waves create changes in space/time and the imbalance of entropy unleashes heat and light.

3) The Bible frequently refers to Christ as the Light. Revelations of God and earthly appearance is through "a light." Each of us can emit light—"Let your light so shine . . ."

4) Speed of light defines the limits of Time and Space.

B. BUT DARKNESS IS real as Phil has found in his life:

Even light can't escape the gravity of a Black Hole (Hell?). But when a Black hole undergoes entropy or collides with another, all that energy is released (End Time?), and light and all the information that was compressed to Singularity breaks out (Victory over Death?).

Space is not empty. Dark Matter, Dark Energy, Gravitational Waves, and Invisible Anti-Matter abound. This reminds us that we don't have to see God in a visible form.

Somewhere in Darkness resides the Devil. Antimatter, negative energy, positive and negative charges, and the Event Horizon of a Black Hole remind us that the Devil could be real in bold contrast to God.

C. THE MYSTERY OF God permeates Phil's thought:

1) So much is not understood by Religion or by Science, but more is continuously being revealed by study of His word and discovered by scientists who continue to explore the Universe. What remains inconsistent is that scientists refuse to acknowledge that the thought that leads to their theoretical physics must be inspired from beyond.

2) Einstein and Hawkins both felt that a God was not needed since the laws of science determine all creation from the "Big Bang" to the end of time. Yet from whence came their thought that led to their discovery? Current thought that nothing existed before the Big Bang and then all after followed Laws, does not explain the origin of "fixed" Law–Ultimate Truth.

3) Not understanding the why and how of Creation, our role in it, and what happens at the end of life does not limit God's control of all three. The search for answers can only bring us closer to God and it certainly appears to be his Will that Ultimate Truth will be revealed in time—His Time.

D. EXPLORING GOD'S MYSTERY can take the form of communication/prayer within which each of us can pursue Truth without offending the Creator by our naivety.

1) Developing a structure that embraces Biblical teaching and is compatible with scientific thought seems more appropriate than separating the two.

2) My concept does not have to be correct or like any other but must be constantly open to God's guidance and Man's correction.

3) Example: Black holes could be Heaven and/or Hell, antimatter could be the devil. Dark energy might be the mode on which communication of waves travel to connect us to the whole (Holy Spirit instructs us in prayer). Matter created from energy after achieving the speed of light squared would explain the Creation, the solar system, and the man/Christ, all coming from one inter-changeable energy and matter source, Himself. Dark matter, that yet to be understood force with gravitational pull and mass unseen, is not only greater than what is in the visible Universe, but fills space and may define that Mystery understandable only through Faith.

E. LIFE IS SHORT but God's time is infinite. Phil reassures us that this is not cause for distress since Faith allows us to share in this timelessness by a life after death:

1) Einstein's Relativity not only expands the relationship of gravity to mass and energy, but blends space and time and reveals how its "warped" nature introduces ways in which time is relative. Scientists believe time and nothing existed prior to the Big Bang and nothing will exist when singularity is again reached. They also believe that time travel and going back in time is possible. But they can't explain from whence came that extremely compact origin of the Big Bang. They can explain backing up time but have no explanation for revelation and prophecy looking into the future.

2) Time can be contracted to nothing since it is affected by gravity and quantum mechanics. We just don't know for sure if

gravity, as we understand it from Newton, matches up with quantum theory. Scientists can't explain this and yet they persist in believing in "predictable" laws of nature without acknowledging who set these laws in motion.

3) The Uncertainty Principle (Heisenberg) puts a hole in the ability to observe speed of a particle (time) and position in time without one observation negating the accuracy of the other. This challenges the Scientific Approach using man's reason. Scientists still haven't resolved this and yet they persist with theoretical physics while lacking "lab" proof.

F. AT THE END of life, what is more important: Knowing who or what God is or what His or Her will for us is?:

1) We can know the will of God through Jesus' teaching—the RED letters in the New Testament.

2) We will know the nature of God through the human form Christ takes and that His forgiveness and grace will be consistent after death—so what is the hurry.

3) After a lifelong quest to pigeonhole God or maybe even create Him in our image, we should be content that He, She or It ("I Am" of the OT) exists and can communicate by all these magnificent waves, particles, and quanta of energy we continue to have unveiled for us, with or without the help of Science.

4) A life of enjoying His Creation and by being completely awed in it each day, comforts any lack of confidence in His purpose.

— Dr. Frederick Reed
65 Lenwood Blvd.
Charleston, SC 29401

www.ingramcontent.com/pod-product-compliance
Lightning Source LLC
Chambersburg PA
CBHW071222090426
42736CB00014B/2934